The 30 Day Prosperity Program

No part of this book may be reproduced or utilized in any form or by any means, electronic or mechanical, including photocopying and recording, or by any information storage or retrieval system, without prior written permission from the author except in the case of "fair use" as brief quotations embodied in critical articles and reviews.

The information contained in this book is for general information purposes only. The author does not dispense or prescribe any medical advice or any technique as a form of treatment for any medical, emotional or physical condition without the advice of a licensed physician, either directly or indirectly. We make no representations or warranties of any kind, express or implied, about the completeness, accuracy, reliability, success, suitability or availability with respect to the information contained in the book for any purpose. Any reliance you place on such information is therefore strictly at your own risk.

Book cover design: Jelena Mirkovic and Astrid Weingärtner
Interior Design: Astrid Weingärtner
Back cover photo: Paul Gregory

Copyright 1st Edition © 2012 Kristie Reeves
Copyright 2nd Edition © 2017 Kristie Reeves
All rights reserved.

ISBN: 1-9384-5101-5
ISBN-13: 9781938451010

The 30 Day Prosperity Program

Kristie Reeves

Beurin Publishing
2nd Edition

Dedicated to my wonderful parents

CONTENTS

Acknowledgements 1
Preface 5
Introduction 9
How to do this program 13
Meditation 17
Day 1: Beliefs about money 19
Day 2: Making a commitment 23
Day 3: Remembering your childhood..............27
Day 4: Ancestral beliefs about money............31
Day 5: Group consciousness 35
Day 6: Religious beliefs about money..............39
Day 7: "Making money is hard" 43
Day 8: Transforming fears....................................47
Day 9: Procrastination 51
Day 10: Secondary gain 55
Day 11: Change your thoughts.........................59
Day 12: Conscious language 63
Day 13: Accountability...67
Day 14: Forgiveness 71

Day 15: Letting go of resentments 75
Day 16: Choosing the positive 79
Day 17: Giving up control 83
Day 18: Having it all 87
Day 19: Where does my money come from? . 91
Day 20: A new prosperity concept 95
Day 21: Changing your focus 99
Day 22: A new sense of prosperity 103
Day 23: Living your truth 107
Day 24: Making money with what you love .. 111
Day 25: Stepping into you power 115
Day 26: Letting your own light shine 119
Day 27: A childlike attitude 123
Day 28: Divine trust 127
Day 29: Unlimited possibilities 131
Day 30: Manifesting your future 135
Continuing your journey 139
Prologue 141
Affirmations 143
About the author 147

Acknowledgements

Life is an amazing journey. I would like to express my gratitude to the people who have been an important part of my journey so far.

To my wonderful and amazing family: Thank you everyone for being there. Mom and Dad—the best parents one could wish for—thank you for your nurturing and love, and for providing the foundation and support to be myself; Steffen- thank you for being my brother; my grandma Margarete, thank you for your wisdom and kindness; my cousin Markus, thank you for providing me with my first teaching space and for all the long talks about life. And thank you, Silke, for being there with us. Thank you to my cousin Astrid for your continued support.To my beautiful friends: Thank you, Kirsten, Marc, Gerhard, Dana, Mara, Jara, Amanda, and Richard for always believing in me; my friend Astrid for the all the late-night conversations at the Naam in Vancouver; Dorothy Becker, for all the support. And thank you to the Divine Source, that Divine Spark that exists in every one of us!

"Follow your heart as it knows your way"

Preface

We know our thoughts create our reality. Whatever we think, whatever beliefs we hold in our conscious or unconscious mind, will reflect as our reality. If we have beliefs of lack and deprivation, exactly that will manifest in our life. If we have thoughts of abundance and prosperity, exactly that will manifest as well.

Having travelled around the globe and meeting people from all kinds of different cultural as well as religious backgrounds, I have found that many were holding the same or very similar beliefs about money and prosperity on the subconscious and even conscious level. There seemed to be a universal theme, and yet this topic seemed very complex at the same time.

What we needed was a way to uncover patterns, unconscious beliefs and emotions and to change whatever was holding us back. We needed to find a way to create thoughts of unlimited possibilities and abundance.

The exercises and meditations in this book are a result of creating this process. I have seen people change their beliefs and thereby transform their lives. I have seen them move from jobs that they despised to work that fulfills them and pays well. I have seen people get out of debt and move into financial abundance. I have seen them start successful businesses, move across the country to start anew, or go back to school to get another degree. And the interesting thing was that the money to embark on these ventures always showed up.

I know that this program can bring you the changes that you desire for your life. This program is not about creating a lot of wealth in a short period of time. It is about creating a completely new concept about money and prosperity. It is about clearing out what no longer serves you and moving into a space where every part of your life is filled with joy and happiness. It is about becoming the master of your own life.

I encourage you to make a commitment to the work, to yourself, and to following these exercises daily. Making a commitment to doing the work and showing up daily will help you to commit to creating the changes necessary to bring in prosperity.

This program is for you. It is supposed to be fun, motivating, and helpful to your growth. Don't do it for your parents, your spouse, your third grade teacher, or to prove yourself. Do it because you know that you are a Divine spark and that you deserve a life filled with abundance, joy, happiness, and prosperity.

I am looking forward to going on this journey with you.

In love and light!

Kristie

Introduction

We create our reality through our thoughts. Whatever thoughts we choose will reflect themselves as our experiences. The things we are experiencing right now, the people who are in our life right now, and our monetary position right now are that way because of thoughts we had in the past and have in the present moment. You might ask now, "So all I need to do in order to create abundance is to change my thoughts, right?" That's right. "But if it is that easy, why haven't I been able to manifest abundance so far, even though I really desire it?"

The thing is that many of our thoughts are stored on the unconscious level and we are not even aware that we have these beliefs. We might consciously think that we deserve to receive all the abundance we desire, but our unconscious mind might think something else. Our unconscious mind is quite powerful. It covers about 88-94 percent of our brain activity (compared to the conscious mind, which covers only about 6-12 percent) and therefore determines most of our life. It stores experiences we have had and things we have learned since we were conceived. It stores belief systems of the collective consciousness as well as experiences and beliefs that are passed on to us from our ancestors through our DNA. It also stores information (memories, experiences and beliefs) from past lifetimes. In order to realize what is holding us back, we need to find out what these beliefs are and change them.

When the so-called recession hit the United States and then the rest of the world in 2009, I knew that it was up to me whether to allow the financial market to affect me or not. I also knew that whatever I chose to believe about the financial situation in the world would create the financial circumstances in my own world. If I allowed fear to take over, if I allowed myself to be dragged into the group consciousness of financial lack, I would soon find myself struggling. But if I kept being aware of my conscious as well as my unconscious thoughts about money, keeping them positive and focused on a prosperity consciousness, I could live in abundance no matter what was going on around me. One of the questions I asked myself was: Why does it seem so easy for some people to create prosperity, and why does it seem so hard for others? What is it that keeps a limit on our abundance?

I realized that I had to start looking at the various aspects of money and prosperity: What do people believe about money? What is money? What does genetics, as well as group consciousness and religion teach about money? How can you move from a place of deprivation to a place of joy and acceptance when it comes to money? I had to create a new and positive approach to money. We live in an abundant Universe and it is for us to realize that we are part of this abundance.

Over the next thirty days we will be exploring your concepts about money and prosperity. This program will make you aware of your conscious and unconscious programs, and it will help you change them. We will find out what is preventing you from manifesting abundance and you will learn how to manifest what you desire. You will create new thoughts and beliefs that are aligned with an unlimited prosperity consciousness which in return will allow you to accept the abundance available to you and everyone else. When making these changes, it is important to keep an open heart and to be ready for miracles. The abundance might not come the way you envisioned it, because the Universe might have had something much better in store for you or a much easier and more joyful way than you had imagined.

Look for synchronicities and act on them. I have seen many people do wonderful work with affirmations and changing belief patterns, but when opportunity knocked on the door, they kept that door closed. Opportunity can be scarier than staying stuck, because opportunity requires responsibility. It is not enough to affirm that you are abundant; action has to follow. If you do thirty days of positive affirmations but make no changes in your daily habits or in the way you live your life, the old belief system can re-create itself. It is important when changing your beliefs to look at how you can incorporate the "new" beliefs into your daily life.

How to do this program

WHAT DO I NEED?

The exercises and meditations require about fifteen to twenty minutes of your time each day. Make sure to set that time aside. Find a comfortable and quiet space in your house where you will not be interrupted. Have a notebook and a pen ready for the exercise part. If you would like to, take a few moments after the daily meditation to write down any additional thoughts that might come up.

WHEN SHOULD I DO THE EXERCISES?

The best time to do these exercises is either first thing in the morning or right before going to bed. The use of the delta and theta brain waves during our sleep cycle allows us to access the unconscious mind and to incorporate new thought patterns with ease if we do the exercises right after waking up or before going to sleep. Each day also has an affirmation that you can repeat several times before going to bed at night (either by reading it out loud or writing it down), so your mind will be able to integrate it while you are sleeping.

DO I NEED TO HAVE ANY PRIOR EXPERIENCE WITH MEDITATION?

No. This program is designed for the beginner as well as for the advanced student. The daily meditations are very simple to follow. The next chapter will give you a suggested meditation. This specific meditation is not mandatory, though. If you have any other technique that you would like to use, feel free to do so.

IS THIS PROGRAM BOUND TO A SPECIFIC BELIEF SYSTEM?

The program is not bound to any religion or specific spiritual practice. You will find me talking about the Divine Source, but feel free to substitute with whatever word you are using for the Divine: God, Allah, Buddha, Christ, Shiva, Yahweh, Great Spirit, Source, Energy, Divine Love, or the Universe.

If you enjoy working with the angels, you might want to ask for their assistance as well. It is your belief in this Divine Energy that will help you grow and change during the process.

Most of all, have fun. Do the program without judging who you are and what you did or didn't do. Your experiences were part of your journey. Know that you can redirect that course any time you choose. Be open to receiving. Be open to the changes that are coming into your life!

Meditation

There are many ways of doing the meditation part of this program. You might have studied some techniques and might want to use what feels familiar to you. The following is a suggested meditation and breathing exercise that you can use to ease yourself into a relaxed state before starting the daily meditation.

Sit down in a comfortable position. Make sure that you have this time for yourself and that no one will distract you. Close your eyes and center yourself in your heart chakra, which is located at the base of your sternum. Take a deep breath and connect to the peace and love that exist in this chakra. Exhale and let go of anything that is on your mind, anything that might worry you or distract you from experiencing the serenity of this moment. As you inhale again, feel the emotion of peace flowing into your physical and emotional body. Repeat the breathing several times, inhaling peace and serenity and exhaling stress and worries, until you feel centered and peaceful.

Now move your attention to your crown chakra, which is located directly above your head. The crown chakra is your opening to the Divine Energy. Imagine a ray of white light from your crown chakra connecting you to the love of creation. This energy is pure unconditional love. Take a deep breath in and hold that breath for a few seconds. With this breath feel the love being strengthened, the colors of the ray becoming lighter and more vibrant and radiating with Divine love.

As you exhale, imagine this Divine energy flowing into your physical body as well as into your electromagnetic field, the energetic force field around your body. Hold the breath again for a few seconds and feel what that energy feels like. Repeat this breathing sequence several times, until you feel at complete peace and relaxation. Feel the energy of Divine love vibrating in your body.

Then move on to the daily meditation.

Day 1: Beliefs about money

In order to begin your journey to prosperity, you first need to find out where you are right now. Each of us has a belief system that is shaped in many ways: by the group consciousness of the society we live in; by beliefs that we took on from our parents, ancestors, teachers, friends, peer group, coworkers, religious or spiritual community; and by the experiences we have had since we came into this world. Our DNA and RNA stores memories and beliefs, as well as emotions from past lives. All these different aspects determine the way we view the world, both consciously and unconsciously. They determine what our life looks like and the kinds of people, places, and circumstances we attract. Depending on these beliefs, we will attract either abundance or lack.

Let us take a look at some of those beliefs. To find out what might be preventing you from manifesting abundance, ask yourself the following questions and write down the first thought that comes to your mind. When you are done, look back at your answers. Do you see a through line or theme to your responses?

- What did my parents teach me about money?
- What does the society I live in/grew up in think about money?
- What did my childhood look like when it came to money?
- Do I believe that it is hard to make money? If so, who taught me that?
- Do I believe that a "real" job can't be fun? If so, why?
- What would happen if I worked a job that was fun? Would I be able to make money with it? Would people respect me for it? Would I respect myself for it? Would my family still love me?
- Would I feel guilty if I had more money than my family/ancestors? Would I feel that I was betraying them?
- Do I believe that money is the root of all evil?
- Do I believe that good people are poor, and rich people are bad?
- Do I belief that being broke/poor is a virtue?

- What did my religion or spiritual beliefs as well as the one of my ancestors teach me about money?
- Do I believe that money will disconnect me from my family and friends?
- Do I feel guilty about having abundance while others live in poverty?
- Do I believe that I have to make a choice between being abundant and being spiritual? That one excludes the other?
- Do I believe that I have to make a choice between being abundant and being loved? Do I believe that I can only be truly loved if I am poor, and that if I am rich, people will only love me for my money?
- Do I believe that I have to make a choice between being abundant and being happy? Do I believe that I can only be happy if I am poor?

Can you see what beliefs are still holding you back? Write down any other thoughts about money that come up. We will work with these beliefs over the next thirty days.

Meditation and Exercise:

Close your eyes. Imagine yourself surrounded by a beautiful white light. Create a visual image of what money looks like to you. Then see a beautiful golden light surrounding that money and filling it with the vibration of unconditional love. What does that new energy feel like to you? What would you like to believe about money? Feel yourself opening up to new thoughts of abundance. Feel this energy filling up your physical body and your auric field. Keep that new feeling throughout the day. Open your eyes and take up your notebook. Write down this statement: "From now on, I believe that money is..." Fill in the blanks.

Affirmation: "I now let go of any old concepts and beliefs about money that no longer serve me. I allow myself to be guided to new thoughts and beliefs about money and prosperity that are aligned with my highest good."

Day 2: Making a commitment

"Until one is committed, there is hesitancy, the chance to draw back - concerning all acts of initiative (and creation), there is one elementary truth that ignorance of which kills countless ideas and splendid plans: that the moment one definitely commits oneself, then Providence moves too. All sorts of things occur to help one that would never otherwise have occurred. A whole stream of events issues from the decision, raising in one's favor all manner of unforeseen incidents and meetings and material assistance, which no man could have dreamed would have come his way. Whatever you can do, or dream you can do, begin it. Boldness has genius, power, and magic in it. Begin it now." (Goethe)

In order to be loved, you have to commit to loving yourself. In order to be happy, you need to commit to creating happiness for yourself. In order to have prosperity, you need to commit to receiving it. All ventures, if they are to be successful, require a commitment.

It is often fear - the underlying question of "What would happen if..." - that prevents us from manifesting the life we want. We fear the good as well as the bad, and most often we fear the good more than the bad.

When doing any kind of work it is important to make a commitment to it and to follow it all the way through. Whatever fears come up, whatever doubts come up, the most important thing is to show up and keep moving forward. The commitment to show up can overcome many doubts and roadblocks along the way. Many times the journey might seem tedious. Many times it seems as if your abundance will never come and your dreams are hitting a roadblock right before they manifest. And many times you might be running out of patience. But it might not be the right timing for you yet. Other things might need to be taken care of before your dreams and your abundance can manifest.

If you're aligned with your Divine Path though and commit to it 100 percent, things will fall into place sooner or later. Commit to focusing on your goal, commit to focusing on the abundance, commit to clearing up any negative beliefs, and the abundance will come!

Above all, make the commitment. I don't know how many exciting and wonderful ideas have been given up too soon, and perhaps right before they would have manifested.

An actor friend of mine gave up a successful theater acting career in New York in order to move to Los Angeles and manifest her dream of being a film actor. She came out here, and things weren't happening the way she thought they would. She was struggling and broke and very frustrated, so she decided to move back to the East Coast. The day she was supposed to fly back to NYC she got called in for an audition and booked the job. Things fell into place and she has become a very successful actress in Los Angeles.

Meditation and Exercise:

Take your notebook and write down the following statement: "I hereby commit to aligning myself with my Divine Path. I commit to receiving abundance and prosperity." Sign it.

Close your eyes and feel yourself surrounded by the unconditional love of the Divine. What does this commitment feel like? Allow any fears or doubts that might come up be replaced or with unconditional love.

Write the statement on a piece of paper and post it on your mirror. Carry it around in your wallet. Do whatever works for you. Make the commitment!

Affirmation: "I hereby commit to receiving the abundance I desire."

Day 3: Remembering your childhood

Many of our beliefs that determine the way we live our life are shaped during our childhood. Children see parents, teachers, and many other adults as authority figures, and we are taught that authority figures are always right; or at least that we need to listen to them and follow their advice. But it was through their own learning and their own experiences that these authority figures shaped their beliefs - some of them inspiring, some of them limiting.

"Making money is hard," "It is impossible to make money that way," "Money doesn't grow on trees," "All artists are poor," "You're not good enough," "You will never amount to anything if you do things your way," and "You need to give up those silly dreams once you grow up" are some of the things authority figures might say. And many people do give up those "silly dreams" that were their passion and might have led them to abundance and prosperity. They pick jobs that are joyless, and they create hardship and struggle when it comes to money.

You have to become clear that these beliefs are other people's opinions, and you don't need to own them or make them your truth. You are not obligated to live your life according to other people's convictions about life or about you. Allow others to have their opinions, but know how discern them from your own inner truth.

☙❧

Meditation:
Let's take a journey into your childhood. Close your eyes and imagine yourself as a little kid: three years old, five years old, seven years old, and nine years old.

What did people tell you about yourself, about what you should do, and about what you can or cannot do? What did people teach you about money? Were their words encouraging or discouraging? Did you listen and follow their advice, even though it might have taken you away from your dreams and your passion? Are you still living your life according to the "good" advice you were given, even though it was against your own better judgment?

Make a list of the beliefs you have taken on and the names of the people who advised you. Then cross out the old beliefs (take a black marker if you have to) and replace them with positive affirmations. Repeat those affirmations during the course of the day and even over the next few days.

Affirmation: "I have discernment between my own truth and the truth of others. I now live my life according to my own inner truth."

Day 4: Ancestral beliefs about money

From the moment we are conceived, we learn. Our parents are usually our first teachers. We learn through the things they tell us, from the way they live their lives, and from the experiences we have with them, and all of this shapes our belief system.

We are also connected to our parents and our ancestral lineage through our DNA. The DNA carries beliefs in the form of physical, emotional, and cellular information that is passed on from generation to generation. Often these beliefs or patterns go many generations back.

Children will also take on their family's beliefs in order to feel connected and loved, or to prove their love to their parents and ancestors. Children might feel that they are betraying their ancestors if they choose a better or different life. They might feel that they have to carry the ancestors' burdens in order to save them. This often happens unconsciously, no matter whether the relationship with the family is a loving one or if the family members have been estranged.

Look at the history of your ancestors. What was your ancestors' relationship to money? What kind of jobs were they working? Where did they live and what happened historically during their lifetime? Did they live during the time of the Great Depression? Did they live during times of war and thus had to experience lack and deprivation? Did they have to battle any drought or famine? What did your parents teach you about money? How did your parents handle money? How did your parents earn their money?

Your ancestor's journey might look quite different from what you imagined for your own life. And that is ok. Know that you can be a part of your lineage and honor your ancestors even if you choose a different path than they did.

Meditation:
Close your eyes and imagine your ancestors standing right in front of you. Acknowledge each one of them. Give gratitude for being a part of the family and thank them for teaching you the things you were allowed to learn. Thank your parents for bringing you into this world.

Visualize any kind of chords between yourself and your ancestors being transformed into unconditional love. Feel the freedom of letting go of these chords.

Affirmation: "I love my family and ancestors unconditionally. I am now free to walk my own path and still honor my ancestors."

Day 5: Group consciousness

Every country, every culture or subculture, seems to have a different consciousness about money. That consciousness is often based on the political or religious views of that particular country or subculture, its history, and the ongoing economic situation.

When looking at your own beliefs about money it is important to look at the beliefs of the country you were raised in. You also might have to look at the consciousness of the country your ancestors were from. We already learned that information is passed on from our ancestors through our DNA, so the group consciousness they were exposed to can affect you as well.

Your soul chose the country you were born in the same way you chose the family you were born into: to learn whatever you decided to learn in this lifetime. It is important to look at the limiting as well as the supporting group consciousness beliefs of the country you live in. It is also important to realize that you still have the freedom to make your own choices about abundance, no matter which culture you live in. You have the freedom to allow yourself to be restricted by the consciousness of the country you live in, as well as its economic situation, or create an abundance consciousness independent of what society dictates to you. You are the one who makes that decision.

୶୶

Meditation:
Close your eyes and take a look at the country and society you live in. What did it teach you about money? What positive things did you learn about money? What limiting or negative beliefs did you take on from the group consciousness?

Let's do some spring cleaning!

Imagine all these beliefs stacked up right in front of you. Go through them and choose which ones you would like to keep and which ones you would like to throw out. Imagine the "old ones" dissolving and the ones that support you expanding and filling that space.

Take a moment to feel that new energy.

Affirmation: "I now choose the beliefs and thoughts that support my ever-expanding abundance consciousness."

Day 6: Religious beliefs about money

Throughout history, humanity has created many religious concepts about money. Poverty, sacrifice, and suffering were talked about as virtues. We were taught beliefs about money such as "Money is the root of all evil," "You have to be poor in order to be close to God," "It is impossible to have money and be spiritual at the same time," "You have to choose between money and a spiritual life - you can't have both," and "God loves the poor and hates the rich."

Many religions and spiritual traditions have been teaching that in order to find a connection with God one has to live in poverty and deprivation. They have been teaching that this is the way back to God - and that it is the only way. No matter what kind of faith you grew up with, these beliefs might also have been transferred to you from your ancestors through your DNA. They might be a group consciousness belief or a past life memory.

In the consciousness of Oneness, we are one with the Divine, and prosperity is part of that Oneness. People can choose to live without material abundance or possessions, but it should be a choice instead of a necessity in order to feel close to the Divine.

The Universe is abundant, and abundance is a gift from the Divine. By denying ourselves this gift, we are denying the Divine and thereby our own Divinity. There is no need to suffer or to be poor in order to be connected to the Divine. We are part of Divinity and therefore always connected to the Divine, always have been, and always will be.

ॐ

Meditation:
Close your eyes for a moment and meditate on the beliefs you have learned regarding what God thinks about money, and on what you believe God would think of you if you were abundant.

Do you believe that poverty is your only way back to God? That deprivation is a virtue?

Do you believe that wealth will disconnect you from the Divine and that spiritual people are supposed to be poor? Do you believe that you can either be loved by God or be abundant? Do you believe you can be spiritual and prosperous at the same time? Do you believe that God is abundant? And that God wants you to be abundant as well?

Make a list of all the different spiritual and religious beliefs that have been limiting you. Then close your eyes and imagine these beliefs being transformed into unconditional love.

Feel yourself becoming one with the abundance of the universe. Can you now accept a new consciousness that allows you to receive abundance from the Divine?

Affirmation: "I am always connected to the unlimited abundance of the Universe. I open myself to receiving abundance from the Divine."

Day 7: "Making money is hard"

How many times have you heard that "making money is difficult," "money doesn't grow on trees," or "the only way to make money is through hard work"? Some people believe that if money comes to them easily or through something that is fun and enjoyable, then it is worth nothing. Many people believe that they have to earn their success, and they make themselves go through long work hours without taking any breaks or time for themselves. They are working a job they don't enjoy while being constantly stressed out with deadlines, demands, pressure, competition, and overwork. Many people have been acquiring abundance that way.

But is that really how you want to "spend" your time? Is that really how you want to create prosperity? Wouldn't it be much better to enjoy the work you're doing? Wouldn't it be much better to get up in the morning and look forward to going to work? Wouldn't it be much better to be able to make money in a way that is fun, while the money comes to you with ease and grace?

I have found in my own life that I had times when I took the job because "I needed the money" - at least that's what I believed. Or I was working very hard on a job, putting in lots of energy and long hours only to find out that I was not getting back even half of what I had put out. I have found that the most prosperity has come to me in times when I was passionate and enthusiastic about what I was doing. The moment I enjoyed my work and started trusting in Divine Guidance, I also allowed the money to come to me with ease.

"Follow your bliss with all your heart and the abundance will come!"

ॐ

Meditation:
Close your eyes and imagine yourself receiving money with ease and joy. What kind of feelings come up? Do you feel worthy of

receiving money effortlessly? Do you feel bad about not working hard for the money you're receiving? Are any self-worth issues coming up? Do you believe that if the money comes to you without struggle or hardship, it is worth nothing and you are cheating?

Feel how the old concepts about making money are sitting like a burden on your shoulders. Now visualize this burden being lifted and dissolved into unconditional love. Feel the energy of abundance coming to you now with ease and grace. Enjoy the feeling of effortless abundance.

Affirmation: "Money now comes to me with ease and grace, and through work that is enjoyable and fun and that I am passionate about."

Day 8: Transforming fears

"Be careful what you wish for; you might just get it." There is so much truth in this saying. Often we are more afraid of taking an opportunity than staying stuck. The unconscious mind likes what it knows and dislikes what is unfamiliar. Therefore staying stuck gives us a sense of safety. Even though we might not like what we have, it feels familiar: we know what to expect and what we are dealing with. Taking an opportunity requires change - often, a leap into the unknown, and it is our fear of the unknown that causes us to turn down the very opportunity we have been longing for.

We start wondering how much our life would change; we start worrying about what other people will think of us, or we become afraid of losing the people we care for. We are afraid of the responsibility that might come with the changes and if we will even be able to succeed with what is required. If our unconscious mind is not familiar with the energy of abundance, it might reject it the moment opportunity comes knocking on our door.

Many people desire a more abundant life but are afraid of it at the same time. The antidote to fear is love. It is love that will help us to succeed.

ॐ

Meditation:
Take some time to journal and write down anything you would like to manifest as if there are no limits - because in truth, there really aren't any. Dream big! When you are done, close your eyes. Imagine you have all the abundance you desire. Imagine what your life looks like, what you are doing, how your relationships look. Really tune in and feel it.

Are there any tears coming up? Do you feel that in order to get one thing you have to give up something else? Are you afraid of the responsibility that comes with money? Are there any fears of loss? Are you afraid people will be jealous or love you only for your money? Do you feel that if you have abundance in your life now, you will have to suffer later? Do you feel fulfilled? Become aware of these thoughts and feelings. The fears or negative beliefs coming up are part of why you have not manifested yet what you want.

Now imagine all of those fears and beliefs being transformed into unconditional love. Feel that love becoming so strong that fear has no more space in your energy field. Do that until you feel safe and peaceful.

Go back to the visualization of your manifestation. How do you feel now about manifesting everything?

Affirmation: "It is now safe for me to manifest my dreams and all the abundance I desire.

Day 9: Procrastination

How many times have you said, "I will do that later"? "I will be happy later." "I will be abundant later." "I will work hard first and then enjoy life later." "I will work a job that I hate because it gives me a secure income and retirement benefits, so I can enjoy life when I retire." You might even have had opportunities coming your way and declined them with the excuse that "it's not the right time yet. I am too busy now doing other things," or "I need to wait for the children to be grown up, for my spouse to make more money, for my car loan to be paid off…"

One of the biggest roadblocks to abundance or, as a matter of fact, anything that brings you joy, is procrastination. Procrastination can have many root causes. It is often founded in doubt or judgment. It is founded in the belief that we are not good enough or worthy enough. It is connected to a sense of martyrdom: only once we have suffered enough or paid our dues can we receive our rewards.

Yes, we do want things to manifest in our life; we want the abundance and the success, we want to live our dreams, we want the joy and the love, and yet we keep telling ourselves, "later." And later will always be later and thus might never come.

What would be so bad though in having all the prosperity, joy, love, happiness, and fulfillment that you desire in your life right now? Wouldn't it be great if you could live the life of your dreams right now instead of having to wait for it until "later"?

❧❧

Meditation:
Close your eyes and imagine what you would like to create in your life right now. Imagine your abundance, your wishes, and your dreams in a balloon of light right in front of you. That balloon is connected to your heart by a golden thread.

If you have any fears, doubts, judgments or worthiness issues coming up, visualize them being transformed into unconditional love. Do that until you feel a sense of peace.

Then take that thread and start pulling your dreams and wishes toward you and into your heart chakra. Feel the joy and love that come through that manifestation, and allow that feeling to fill up your physical and emotional body. Know that you are safe and taken care of.

Affirmation: "I embrace my dreams and my abundance, and I open myself up to receiving my highest good NOW."

Day 10: Secondary gain

Why does it sometimes seem so hard to give up the suffering we are in? Why does it seem so hard to give up the misery? Or the deprivation? The circumstances we do not want? Yes, we do want to create abundance. Yes, we do want things to change, but we still keep holding on to the old. Why? We do it because we are getting something out of it. It is called "secondary gain."

I have seen people who manifested an illness in order to justify their need for love and support. They - often unconsciously - felt unworthy and needed to create a reason for being loved and supported. I have seen people who created constant drama, because they felt this was the only way to have people pay attention to them. I have seen people who created poverty in their lives and needed support from others, because receiving that support finally made them feel taken care of.

As you can see, the lack in our lives - no matter if that lack is on the material, physical, emotional, or spiritual level - can have many secondary gains. People refuse to give up their lack or their illness because they feel they will not be able to get what they desire without it, or because they are afraid of losing the very things they gained by manifesting the lack or illness in the first place. They have not yet learned to receive through positive, joyful, and uplifting ways.

In order to give up your secondary gain, ask yourself how it has served you. What have you been getting out of it?

In order to receive unconditionally and without any secondary gain, you need to start loving, accepting, and appreciating yourself first.

ৎ৵

Meditation:
Close your eyes and ask yourself these questions: Where in my life am I creating lack? How does this lack serve me? What am I

getting out of it? What would I lose if I lost the lack itself? Does the thought of giving up the lack create any fears?

Visualize the energy of Divine love surrounding you. How does that feel? Become one with it. Know you are a spark of this Divine love and therefore always loved, protected, and taken care of. Know that as a Divine spark it is your birthright to live a life filled with prosperity, health, love and joy. Are you now ready lo let go of your secondary gain? If you are, then visualize it being dissolved and transformed into unconditional love.

Bonus exercise: Write a love letter to yourself! If you can learn to truly love and fully accept yourself, you do not need to create negative circumstances to justify your need for prosperity, love, and joy.

Affirmation: "I now live my life according to my own Divinity. I receive the good in my life without any conditions attached to it and without needing to justify it."

Day 11: Change your thoughts

We have probably all been in situations where we felt stuck and there seemed to be nothing we could do about it, where we felt other people were treating us unjustly or were completely disregarding our talents and needs; or where we were working very hard, but everything in our surroundings seemed to be against us.

We might remember situations where we were attracting lack instead of the abundance we were wishing for. In those situations, life didn't feel fair. We might have felt victimized by other people or life itself and possibly asked, "What did I do to deserve this? What did I do wrong?"

Remember that your environment is a reflection of your conscious and unconscious thoughts, emotions and patterns. Nothing in this world happens to us. It happens because of us. It happens because of what we believe and the energy we radiate out into the world, and our environment merely a mirrors that energy.

Everything that is in your life right now is there because of a thought you had in the past. It is your thoughts that created the lack or the abundance in your life. It is your thought patterns that created the way other people are treating you. It is your thoughts that created the circumstances of your current life. And here lies your power: if you were able to create your currently reality with your thought patterns, you have the power to change it by changing your thoughts.

Once we start recognizing our environment and our relationships as a mirror of our own thought patterns, we can quickly find out what these patterns are and change them. That might be a really big concept, but once you get it, you will be able to become the master of your own life and start creating the reality that you desire!

Meditation:

Take a look at your life the way it is right now. How do your circumstances make you feel? Which parts of your life do you dislike? What would you like to change? What kind of beliefs are the people around you reflecting back to you? What kind of thought patterns could have created your current life circumstances?

Take your notebook and make a list of all the beliefs and thoughts that come up. Once you are done, turn any negative beliefs and feelings into positive statements that you can use as affirmations. Close your eyes and repeat the positive affirmations several times while visualizing how your life will change for the better.

Affirmation: "I am choosing to become the master of my own life. I now choose thoughts that support the good in my life."

Day 12: Conscious language

When changing our prosperity consciousness it is very important that we become aware of our words and thoughts. The language we use is more powerful than we often realize. A statement, either spoken out loud or as a thought, when repeated often enough will manifest itself as a belief or thought pattern in our unconscious mind and start creating exactly that reality around us.

Many language patterns, phrases, and expressions are so ingrained into us that we frequently use them without realizing what we are saying. Changing your life often means learning a new language, a language that is based on positive thought, possibility, and a limitless way of thinking.

How often have you used the phrase "I can't afford that"? How often have you said, "I will try to make more money"; "I will try to find a better job"; "I will try to change my life"? As long as you just "try," nothing will happen - you need to go out and do it.

True, you might not have the money in your bank account at the moment to take that dream vacation of yours, or buy the car, or the house. The new job might not have shown up yet. But by reaffirming that you "cannot afford" it, you will stay in a state of lack. By reaffirming that it is hard to create a change, you will make it difficult for yourself to bring about the shifts you are longing for.

Become aware of the words you are choosing. Keep affirming that you "can afford" it and the abundance will show up. Keep affirming that "it is possible", and the possibilities will come your way. Choose your words clearly, so that they will support what you would like to create.

ॐ

Exercise:
Task for today: Keep your journal or a piece of paper with you throughout the day. Take this day to really become aware of the

words you are using. Write down any phrases that are preventing you from manifesting what you would like to have. Write down any phrases you are saying that are preventing you from living in abundance.

At the end of the day, look at your list. Turn the phrases into positive affirmations that will help you manifest your dreams, and work with these affirmations.

Affirm: "I choose my words and thoughts wisely and according to my highest and best good."

Day 13: Accountability

As the consciousness is rising on this planet, we are becoming more and more aware that we have the choice to create our lives according to our dreams and visions. We are becoming more and more aware how powerful we are as co-creators through our actions and thoughts. And with possibility comes accountability.

In the past we were often taught that "you have no other option"; "that this is just how things are and you have to accept them," and that "there is nothing you can do about it." Societal structures and group consciousness pre-determined the way our life looked like. We had to "follow the rules" of who to marry, which job to choose, how much abundance we could create and how to organize our life. We had to take the place in society determined by our ancestral lineage.

As we are liberating ourselves from these

old structures, we have to retrain our muscle of taking responsibility for our life. We have to re-learn to make our own choices. Where other people would make the decisions for us in the past, we are now being asked to choose and create for ourselves.

This can be overwhelming at times. We might start wondering if we are on the right path and whether we will be able to succeed. We might become fearful of other peoples' or even our own expectations of ourselves. We might doubt the choices we are making or judge the progress we made. And we start wondering if it wouldn't be easier to go back to having someone else make these decisions for us and thereby take the responsibility for their outcome.

Self-love and self-acceptance are the keys to taking accountability. If you love yourself enough, no "mistake" or "failure" will make you doubt yourself. If you love yourself enough, you will automatically be guided to making the decisions that are in alignment with your highest good.

What if you knew you couldn't fail? What if you knew that no matter what the outcome would be, you'd still and always be loved? What if failure and mistakes didn't exist? What if you knew that you are divinely cared for? What if you knew that anything is possible and that everything you need in order to manifest your dreams is already available for you? Does accountability still look and feel like such a big and scary thing?

Meditation:
Close your eyes and think of all the situations where you didn't follow through on an opportunity because you were afraid of the accountability that came with it, or situations where you blamed yourself for failing. Look at all these situations without judgment and see them as a learning experience. Imagine the situation and everyone involved surrounded by white light, and visualize any blame, shame, anger, and regret being transformed into unconditional love.

Go into your heart center and feel

unconditional love emanating from your heart into your whole being. Know that this love is a part of you and you cannot lose it, no matter what.

Then visualize what you would like to manifest and how it would feel to be abundant and to be working in a job that fulfills you. Does it feel safe now to become accountable for your life? What can you do, in order to take charge of your life? Make a list. Pick one thing and do it this week.

Affirmation: "I am divinely guided, loved, and protected, and it is safe for me to be accountable for my life."

Day 14: Forgiveness

Forgiveness is a very important step on the way to prosperity. As long as we are unable to forgive, we are not free to fully enjoy our life, manifest our dreams and step into our Divine Abundance.

If you are unable to forgive certain situations, people, or even yourself, you will most likely re-create the same patterns. Unforgiveness creates a chord that keeps us connected to the "old" situations, patterns and the people we are holding grudge against. Unforgiveness means that you haven't released the emotion or the person associated with the situation. The unconscious mind then accepts the hurt as its new reality and will continue to create more of that same feeling by attracting similar situations over and over again.

The Hawaiian Kahunas teach that forgiveness is the key to liberation. Forgiveness brings healing and the freedom to create your life anew. I have seen it many times that people wanted to create something new and positive, and yet they kept re-creating the same old painful patterns. They kept attracting people who reminded them of past hurts. They kept attracting similar circumstances over and over again. It was not until they forgave the situation and everybody involved in it (including themselves) that they were able to free themselves from the past.

You can change the old patterns by looking at people and situations you have yet been unable to forgive. Forgive the other person as well as yourself and you will be able to witness a new sense of freedom that will allow you to move forward and manifest what you desire.

※

Meditation:
In your notebook, make a list of people you feel you need to forgive - you might have to include yourself as well. Then make a list of situations and circumstances you need to forgive.

Once the list is done, close your eyes and go through it one name or one situation at a time. Imagine the person standing in front of you. If it is a situation, imagine the situation. Then say "I love you. I forgive you. I now release you to your own higher good."

Affirmation: "I now release the past. I forgive myself and everybody else involved. I move forward in peace."

Day 15: Letting go of resentments

As with unforgiveness, resentments keep us stuck in the past. We often hold on to resentments as a security mechanism: they remind us of what went wrong, so we won't repeat the same mistake again. Many times resentments serve as a boundary between ourselves and another person, especially if the other person is associated with pain or hurt in some form.

I have seen people who were unable to manifest their dreams because if they did, they would resent the fact that they hadn't done it earlier, or they would resent the person who told them not to do it in the first place.

Others are holding on to resentment to prevent people from coming too close to them, because past experiences have taught them that closeness isn't safe, but it is this very distance that prevents them from receiving the love and support they would need to manifest their dreams.

Whatever the reason, resentments put walls around us that prevent abundance from flowing into our life. Becoming aware of resentments and how they have served you so far will give you the ability to look at the situation that created the resentment and release it. Releasing it will help you regain your sense of freedom, along with an increased sense of safety.

Releasing resentments will also allow you to view the situation from a different perspective. You will be able to see the lessons behind it and learn from them, and be able to react differently the next time a similar situation comes around.

You will be able to set new boundaries and say no before you get hurt. You will also create the space you need to allow people into your life who will nurture, love and support you unconditionally.

Meditation:

Let's take a look at the past and the future. Close your eyes and think of your life right now. What and who do you resent from the past? Imagine if you had everything that you'd like to manifest in your life: what and who would you resent, if you did? Are those resentments keeping you safe? Are they teaching you any lessons? Do you need to hold on to them in order to not get hurt again? Is the resentment your way of creating strong boundaries?

Tune in and feel where in your body the resentments are present. Once you have identified them, visualize white light flowing into these area and transforming any kind of resentment into unconditional love.

Ask to cut the chords that are connected to the resentments—to the people, places, and situations. See those chords leaving you and going to the light. Witness healing energy and white light filling up the areas where the chords used to be attached and where the resentments used to be stored.

Experience the new sense of freedom that comes from releasing these attachments.

Affirmation: "I now let go of any and all resentments that are still holding me back. I am safe without them. I am free."

Day 16: Choosing the positive

Have you seen the movie Pretty Woman? If you did, you might remember the scene where Vivian (Julia Roberts's character) tells Edward (Richard Gere's character) that it has always been easier for her to accept the negative things that people said about her than the positive ones.

Why is it that we choose the negative over the positive so many times? Why is it so much easier for us to accept a negative remark about ourselves than a compliment? How many times have you brushed aside a compliment? Our choice to accept the negative over the positive seems to be based on one common emotion: the feeling of rejection.

We have been put into a place of mistrust, by negative programming and experiences from childhood; poverty consciousness; the fear that we might owe another person something if we accept a gift or even a compliment; past betrayals or hurts; self-doubt and self-denial. We have stopped trusting that the good that is right in front of us will actually stay, and that we are worthy of it. We doubt that the good is a gift from the Divine and ours to accept without any obligations, so we continue rejecting the good before it can reject us.

It is hard to manifest abundance if you are running a pattern of rejection, if you don't know how to trust, how to follow your instincts, or how to follow Divine Guidance. In order to move into a place of prosperity, you will have to move from rejection to acceptance. Once you love yourself the way you are and learn how to trust yourself, rejection will fall out of the equation. Trusting and loving yourself will guide you into the right direction; you will know what steps to take and what opportunities to choose, and you will finally be able to accept the gifts of abundance the Universe has in store for you.

Meditation:

Take a moment right now and close your eyes. Think of a situation in the past where you declined an opportunity or a gift that was offered to you, only to regret it later. In your mind, go back to that point in time, and imagine being offered the gift or the opportunity again. This time, accept it with gratitude. Know that you are worthy and deserving of receiving it. Trust that the gift originates from the Divine. Say "thank you" and feel what that feels like.

Let's time travel to the future as well. Think of something you would like to manifest in your life. Imagine yourself receiving it. Know that you are worthy and deserving of receiving it. Trust that the gift originates from the Divine. Say "thank you." Feel what that feels like and carry that feeling with you throughout the day.

If you have been calibrated to rejection for a long period of time, you might have to practice acceptance until it feels right for you again. You can start with the little things in your daily life, like getting a great parking spot, a flower that is blossoming right in front of your kitchen window, or someone allowing you to go in front of them at the supermarket checkout line. Once you learn to accept the "small" things with gratitude, it will feel safe to you to say yes to the "big" things as well.

Affirmation: "I am worthy and deserving of receiving good in my life right now."

Day 17: Giving up control

Many times we have thought about what we want. We have created a vision board with images of what we dream about and made a list of things we would like to manifest over the next six months. We have set long-term goals and short-term goals and have pre-meditated on every single step along the way to get to our goals. We are sitting at the starting line ready to go, just waiting for the next step to happen, and, yes, we are working very hard to make that next step happen. So hard! But nothing does happen, despite all our efforts, and we start wondering why.

Often it is because we are set on a specific way for things to happen. We think we know exactly what the next step is, how to go about things, where our money is supposed to come from, and how we want things to manifest. We have decided on a certain way and won't back up no matter how hard it is.

A teacher of mine once said to me: "Stop trying to open locked windows. Instead, go through the door that is already open for you."

And yes! Too often we get stuck trying to open those locked windows, and miss an opportunity, that open door, that is right in front of us. It is absolutely important to have goals and to visualize what you would like to manifest. The key, though, is to not get stuck on just one way to go about it, but to allow possibility to show up in may different ways. Stop micromanaging the Universe. The Universe is abundant and limitless. Maybe the Universe has way more prosperity to offer you than you could have imagined. Maybe the Universe has a much easier and more fun way to bring that prosperity about, and by being so focused on only one way, you might be disconnecting yourself from that opportunity.

The key is to set your goals and start allowing the Divine Truth within to guide you.

Meditation:

Close your eyes and feel yourself completely connected to Divine love and light. Visualize your path right in front of you as a way that is illuminated by this Divine love and light. Let go of any preconceived notions of how to walk that path, and instead, feel yourself stepping into a place of trust, knowing that your inner truth will guide you and support you on that path. What does that feel like? Imagine the energy of this trust fill up your physical and emotional body with a sense of deep peace.

Become aware of synchronicities. Look for signs. Look for that open door. Be open to receiving.

Affirmation: "I now allow myself to be Divinely guided on my life path."

Day 18: Having it all

Many people say they are so focused on their work that they do not have the time to be in a relationship. Others feel they would have to give up an existing relationship in order to follow their passion in their work life. And others were taught that it is impossible to make money with a job that is fulfilling and inspiring. Some people might feel guilty about taking time out for themselves and having fun instead of being focused on work 24/7.

These limiting concepts come from the conviction that it is impossible to have it all: the abundance, the joy, the love, and the happiness. People believe that there is a choice to be made between having one thing or the other; that they would be selfish or even egotistical to have it all. It seems that it would be too much to ask for.

Giving up one thing in order to get something else is based on a lack mentality. It is based on the belief that there is not enough: enough time, enough abundance, enough support, enough for everyone. It is based on the feeling that we are not enough: we do not feel that we deserve happiness in every aspect of our lives. It is based on the fear of being punished if our life is too good, or the feeling of guilt because we might be taking things away from others.

The truth, though, is that the Universe has an unlimited amount of abundance and prosperity, that anything is possible, and that there are no limits to what we can do, have, or manifest.

We deserve to be happy, fulfilled, and abundant, and everyone is worthy and deserving of having it all. You don't serve the world by believing that it is a bad thing to be happy and fulfilled in all aspects of your life; quite the opposite: the more you step into the abundance of fulfillment in all areas of your life, and the more you move into joy and happiness, the more you can affect the world and the people around you in a positive way.

Life is a gift and our purpose is to accept this gift and cherish it. Why not give every day the chance to become the most fulfilled, the most joyful, the most happy and abundant day of your life? If you believe it is possible, then it will be. If you believe you can have it all, you will!

※

Meditation and Exercise:
Close your eyes and imagine what your life would look like to make it abundant, fulfilled and joyful.

How would your life look like if you knew anything was possible and there were no limits? Imagine every single detail of it. Where would you live? Who would be around you? What would you do? How would you feel?

Take your notebook and write down your "perfect life" in every single detail. Write it as if it were already here, as if it was happening today, right now.

Affirmation: "I now believe in a Universe without limits. I open myself up to the opportunity of having all the joy, abundance, happiness, love, (add whatever else you'd like to add to the list) that I desire. I give this day the chance to become the best day of my life so far. I am worthy and deserving of 'having it all'."

Day 19: Where does my money come from?

We are taught that our money comes from our clients, our customers, or our employer. We keep seeking new ways to receive more money by getting more clients, more sales, a better job, or a higher salary. This way of thinking, though, makes us feel dependent on outer circumstances and on other people for our own prosperity. It makes us a slave to money. As long as we believe that money comes to us from external sources, we will allow it to control us.

It is important to remember that everything in this Universe originates from Source Energy. Yes, money will probably be given to you by an employer, a client, or a customer.

What you need to remember, though, is that the money comes through them and not from them. It originated from Source, and since you are a part of this Creation, you are connected to that Source and therefore to the abundance at all times.

The moment you really know that truth, you are free; and you will become the master of your circumstances, knowing that prosperity is always available for you.

☙❧

Meditation:
Close your eyes and imagine a big ball of white light. See yourself within that ball of light. Imagine a second ball of light in front of you and the people or places you are receiving your money through within that second ball of light. Above you is a third ball of light that symbolizes pure Divine Source Energy. Know that this energy has an unlimited amount of prosperity and abundance available for you. Since you are a Divine spark, you automatically are a part of this prosperity and abundance energy field.

Now imagine this abundance flowing from the ball of light that symbolizes the Divine Source Energy through the people or places within the ball of light in front of you and then coming to you. Allow yourself to accept that abundance. Thank the Universe for always providing for you.

Affirmation: "My prosperity originates from the Divine Source Energy. Since I am part of this energy, the abundance of the Universe is always available for me."

Day 20: A new prosperity concept

Money was originally intended as a means of exchange. There was no negative or positive energy or belief associated with it. There was no judgment. Money simply was. Over the course of time, though, the way it was used made humans acquire a new perception of money, one that was often very far away from what it was initially intended to be. Money and prosperity suddenly became associated with something negative.

Instead of money simply being used as a way to pay for things, people started acquiring money and using it to control others, to exploit, to suppress, and to make themselves superior. Money was used as a status symbol; it was used for corruption and started representing an insatiable greed. Money meant power, and that power could be used to undermine and suppress others. To this day, money is still used that way in many instances.

Oftentimes these associations with money will result in people having a hard time making or holding on to money. They want to be a good person, but money means something bad to them. And when money actually does come their way, they will reject it or create circumstances (often unknowingly) to rid themselves of their prosperity.

The times are changing, though, and with it our view of prosperity. It is time for us to take a look at the way we have been using money and replace the old concepts with new ones. What if we started attributing love, respect, equality, acceptance, and support to money? How would your world look with such a money concept?

ൟൟ

Meditation and Exercise:
Close your eyes and create a visual image of money. Imagine the energies of love, respect, and equality (and whatever else you might like to add) filling up and surrounding your image of money. See yourself going out into the world and circulating the kind of

money that has all those positive attributes. See money with exactly that kind of energy returning to you.

Throughout the day, whenever you are receiving or spending money, bless the money, visualize the positive attributes within the money you are giving or receiving. Give gratitude for it.

Affirmation: "I now allow the energies of love, respect, equality and joy to flow into my money and abundance."

Day 21: Changing your focus

How many times have you looked at your life and seen only what you are still missing instead of looking at the blessings you have already received? How many times have you worried about things not falling into place fast enough? How many times have you complained about not having enough time, enough money, or enough happiness?

There is a law in the Universe that says that whatever we focus on will increase. If we focus our attention on the things we don't have (yet), we are programming our unconscious mind and our cellular memory to a state of deprivation and are thereby creating more lack.

Our unconscious mind is like a magnet, and it constantly keeps attracting exactly what it is programmed to. It demands an ongoing "fix" by re-experiencing the emotions and beliefs that it has stored and thus creates circumstances and attracts people that will satisfy that need. If we keep complaining about what we don't have, about things not falling into place fast enough, or people not treating us the way we would like to be treated, the unconscious mind will create more of those experiences in order to fulfill its needs.

The secret to manifesting what we desire is to bless what we have in our life. The moment we shift our focus from lack and deprivation to a feeling of gratitude for the things we do have, the unconscious mind will start creating circumstances that comply with these new emotions. It will start creating its daily "fix" for gratitude and blessings by creating more situations and bringing in more people you are grateful for.

The good things in our life will increase, and thus we start moving into a state of prosperity.

Meditation and Exercise:

In your notebook, write down ten things you are grateful for. Follow this with ten things you have accomplished and that you are proud of.

After you are done with this part of the exercise write a gratitude letter to yourself.

Close your eyes and center yourself in your heart chakra. Give love and gratitude to all the blessings you have received in your life.

Affirmation: "I now focus on the blessings I have received in my life. I am grateful for them."

Day 22: A new sense of prosperity

So many people have been taught that prosperity is only measurable in money or material possessions. They keep chasing bigger houses, more expensive cars, fancier clothes, more fame and recognition, and bigger bank accounts. What they fail to see is how much prosperity is around them and in their life already.

A feeling of prosperity can come to us in many different ways. It does not need to come from the amount of money in our bank account or the number of stocks that we own. It does not need to come from the car we are driving or the house we live in.

We live in a prosperous Universe, and all we need to do is become aware of it. Look at nature. Look at the ocean, the sky. Look at the intricate pattern of a flower and feel and see the prosperity in it.

Prosperity might also be the amazing friends you have in your life. It might be the endless possibilities that are available for you and that you have yet to become aware of. It might be a flower that your child picks for you. Do not just sit around and wait for the "big stuff" to happen - look for the details. Find prosperity in the smallest and most wonderful places. See and feel the abundance that is already around you and available for you - be grateful for it.

Awareness of the abundance you already have, of the prosperity that is always around you, will allow a new flow of prosperity in your life.

ॐ

Meditation and Exercise:
Take your notebook and write down at least ten things that you have in your life already that make you feel prosperous. Add five situations you have experienced that gave you a sense of abundance. Close your eyes and remember the feeling you had when you received all this prosperity. Move into a space

of gratitude. Imagine this feeling filling up your whole body.

What can you do today to add to this feeling of prosperity? Buy yourself a little treat: a special kind of chocolate that you usually would not get for yourself, or a bouquet of flowers. Go to the beach and collect some seashells, or take a bubble bath and light a candle while enjoying it. Prosperity might also mean turning off the phone and taking an hour just for yourself.

Spend your day becoming aware of the abundance that is and has been around you.

Affirmation: "I am aware of the unlimited prosperity in my life. I now see prosperity in the beauty around me."

Day 23: Living your truth

We tend to give up our dreams for many reasons: the need for acceptance, the false idea that others will love us more if we follow their ideas of who we are, the need to please others by living up to their expectations, the fear of failure, and a group-consciousness belief of what is possible and what isn't. We were taught that sacrifice is a virtue, so we sacrifice our own dreams for someone else's. Children will often give up their childhood dreams and follow their parents' ideas in order to prove their love to them.

At the same time we feel miserable, because deep down inside we know what our soul longs for. We feel miserable because we are denying our soul its happiness and joy. We were taught that it is selfish to follow our desires. But desire means from (=de) God (=sire). By rejecting our desires, we reject our gifts from the Divine.

It is time to realize that love is our divine birthright, and that there is nothing we need to do in order to receive it, not even give up our dreams. It is time to stop living our life according to the expectations of others and instead start living our life according to our own inner truth. We need to start becoming independent of what society, group consciousness and the people around us determine is possible or impossible.

Your desires are your roadmap to living your Divine Truth. Whatever you desire, it is already there for you in some form. It is that spark of truth inside of you that points your way. If you didn't have it inside of yourself, how could you know about it, want it, and long for it?

Follow your desires, that inner calling as it will point you to your highest truth.

ळ∞

Meditation:
Close your eyes and look at your life right now. What aspects of it bring you joy and

happiness? Which areas would you like to change or improve? What could you add to your life to increase the joy and happiness in it? What is it that your soul is longing for?

Know that the things you long for, that give you fulfillment and true happiness, are part of your Divine Truth.

Affirmation: "I now give myself permission to follow my inner calling, and to live my life according to my highest truth."

Day 24: Making money with what you love

Far too many people compromise their passions for a safe way to make money. It sometimes seems easier to go for safety than for our dreams. Group consciousness, ancestral beliefs, teachers and peers try to tell us that our dreams are "just dreams" and "impossible to reach", that we should settle for what is "acceptable" or "possible". The opinions, beliefs, and good advice of others can shape a belief system that predetermines our choices on how to make money.

It is these beliefs that prevent us from creating prosperity with what we love. Instead of listening to our heart, we listen to what we have been taught, so that the moment we actually do set foot in the direction of our dreams we seem to fail. Money issues start showing up, and we go back to our safe jobs.

How many times have you stopped yourself from going for your dreams because of the doubts instilled in you? How many times did you want to start your own business, and someone was able to talk you out of it because "there is no money in this" or because "it is too risky." Are you familiar with the "starving artist mentality"? Have you been conditioned to certain ideas about how and with what to make money?

If you allow your life to be predestined by these beliefs, you limit yourself from what you truly want and from what you truly are capable of. Many great ideas have been given up because people were worried that they would not be able to make a living doing what they were passionate about.

The truth, though, is that if you follow your passion and trust yourself, trust that there is a greater force that is providing for you, prosperity will inevitably follow. Many great things have been achieved by people who kept believing in their dreams no matter what.

In the prophet Ezekiel's kabalistic work

known as The Chariot there is a saying that goes, "When a man takes one step toward God, God takes more steps toward that man than there are sands in the worlds of time." Let's take that step now.

༺ ༻

Meditation and Exercise:

Take your notebook and write the following sentence: "I now allow myself to make money with…"

List any ideas, passions, or dreams of how you would like your prosperity to come about. Date it and sign it.

Close your eyes. Imagine yourself in a ball of white light, and ask to be connected to your ideal job with the money you would like to make.

Ask to be connected to the people, places, and circumstances that will support your dream and bring about your job in the highest and best good. Visualize and feel that connection. Feel how your prosperity is now coming through work that fulfills you.

Affirmation: "I now allow myself to receive money and prosperity through a job I love and am passionate about."

Day 25: Stepping into you power

Many people are afraid to step into their own power. There seems to be an underlying distress: a fear of what might happen if they were powerful. They are afraid to use their power as much as they are afraid to misuse their power. Power triggers fears of being controlled and overpowered by others. It triggers memories of (often traumatic) situations where they were negatively affected by the power play of others or where they might have exploited their own power.

The word "power" has many negative beliefs associated with it. As with the concept of money, the original meaning of power was changed through both individual and group-consciousness experiences.

You will be unable to create prosperity and walk your Divine Path as long as you are allowing others to control your life. In order to create prosperity in your life you have to stop giving away your power. You need to move from a human concept of power to a Divine knowledge and understanding of what power really is. You need to give up any and all old beliefs about power that have distorted the truth of what power really is.

Power was never intended to harm, control, or suppress anyone. It was meant for humans to be who they really are and to bring that knowledge and purpose into the world. Power was meant to support the good of everyone.

If you are standing in your Divine Power, you will have that knowledge. You will not allow anyone else to distract you from who you are and what your Divine Purpose is. You will just know and be. You will know that your power is Divinely aligned, and you will know how to use it for the highest and best good for yourself as well as everyone else.

ॐ

Meditation and Exercise:
Take your notebook, and for a moment

meditate on what power means to you. What did the history of the world teach you about power? What did your own experiences, or the experiences of people around you teach you about power? Do you see power as something suppressing and controlling, or as something supporting that is giving you strength?

Write down all the "old" beliefs about power that come up. After you are done with that, write down what Divine Power is and can be for you.

Close your eyes and see yourself surrounded by a beautiful white light. Our solar plexus is our power center and stores many of the memories and emotions associated with power. Focus your energy on your solar plexus. How does that feel? Visualize the healing energy of the Universe transform any traumatic emotions as well as fears that have been stored in your solar plexus. Feel them being transformed into unconditional love. Keep focusing on this area until you feel completely at ease in your power center. Ask to restore your your solar plexus with a concept of Divine Power.

Affirmation: "I now stand in my Divine Power and I know how to use this power in the highest and best good."

Day 26: Letting your own light shine

Guilt can become a major roadblock on the path to prosperity. I hear people say, "Well, it is all very nice that I can learn how to manifest anything I want, but isn't that selfish? How can I enjoy prosperity if so many people in this world are still suffering and living in poverty?"

Here is my question: how can others learn how to be happy, fulfilled, abundant, and prosperous if they have no role model to follow? How can you serve others and help them move into joy and abundance if you are still holding onto suffering or sacrifice? And how do you expect to be able to help others if you live in poverty, suffering, and deprivation?

Many cultures used to regard prosperity as a virtue, because people who had abundance had a duty to help the less fortunate and gained the respect of others by doing so. When some of the recent natural disasters hit, many people came together, collecting money in order to help. They could do so because they had the prosperity to do it. Instead of feeling guilty for having more, they used their abundance to elevate the lives of others.

Once you step away from a feeling of guilt and start lifting your own energy to one of love and prosperity, you will be able to create change in this world. Energy circulates: whatever you are sending out will affect others and come back to you as well. Think about what kind of energy you would like to radiate into this world. What kind of energy would help the world to be elevated to a higher consciousness? What if you lived in a constant state of unconditional love, bliss, joy, happiness, fulfillment, and prosperity? What if you radiated those kinds of emotions into the world?

By allowing yourself to be fulfilled, happy, and prosperous, you become a shining light for other people.

Meditation and Exercise:

Today, write down ten things about yourself that you like, and another ten things that you enjoy doing and that make you happy. Write down ten things that you would like to manifest that you haven't allowed yourself to receive in the past.

Feel the energy, the happiness, the joy you are receiving from having these things in your life. How is your own joy and happiness affecting others? How can you use that joy and happiness to elevate the lives of the people around you?

Close your eyes and visualize how it would feel to be filled with love for yourself and happiness for what you are doing. Imagine these feelings radiating from your heart center into the world.

Affirmation: "I allow myself to let my own light shine."

Day 27: A childlike attitude

"Imagination is more important than knowledge." (Albert Einstein)

Listen to little kids telling you what they want to do when they grow up. There is no limit to what they think they will be able to accomplish, and they will describe it to you in the most vivid and magical colors and details. But the older they get, the more they lose that passion and their belief in unlimited possibilities. They conform to what is expected of them and listen to other people's ideas of what is possible instead of living their dream. Sound familiar?

As people grow up, they become rational instead of imaginative. Our work becomes reasonable instead of memorable. We are taught that our childhood dreams belong to our childhood, and that it is time to grow up and behave like an adult. We are taught that work is not supposed to be fun; and if it is fun then it is not really work. We are taught to operate within the paradigm of a "mature" adult, and instead of being inspired (in spirit), we play it safe.

I believe that our childhood dreams are signposts to our Divine Purpose. A childlike attitude of wonder and excitement can help us discover untraveled roads. It is from that childlike attitude and imagination that magic happens. Instead of allowing us to conform, it will lead us to who we are, to our true gifts and authenticity.

Have the audacity to be authentic! Prosperity follows inspiration and authenticity!

ॐ

Meditation and Exercise:
Take a journey into your past. Make a list by answering the following questions: What did you dream about doing when you were a little kid? What excited you? What were the most fun things you used to do? Then make another list. What are you dreaming of doing right now? What are you passionate about? What would make you happy? What would you

need to do in order to feel fulfilled? What would you do if you allowed yourself to have fun? Are there any dots between your childhood dreams and your current dreams that you can connect?

Close your eyes. Let go of any expectations, any have tos, shoulds, or musts. Visualize being connected to your dreams and desires. Allow yourself to feel the joy and fun of it. Feel the energy of the Universe supporting you in every single step you take.

Affirmation: "I am now connected to my own authentic self. I allow a childlike attitude and curiosity guide me to my Divine Purpose and prosperity."

Day 28: Divine trust

The antidote to fear is trust. Whatever fears and insecurities you may be facing on your path to prosperity, you will be able to overcome once you step into a place of trust. This is often easier said than done, though. It seems to be very hard for many people to step into a place of trust.

The problems are disappointments and even traumas that are associated with trust. They might be our own past experiences: things we learned from our family, our ancestors, society, or history. How many times have you trusted someone and then been betrayed, abandoned, or let down? How many times have you been told that you can trust no one and should rely only on yourself? How many times have you seen people misuse another's trust?

Experiences we had in the past as well as group consciousness we grew up with have shaped our understanding of what trust is. The Divine understanding of trust is that you can fully and completely rely on something or someone, and that you can have absolute faith in the support and integrity of that thing or person. Divine trust means that you are 100 percent connected to the Divine and thereby taken care of at all times.

In order for us to receive prosperity we need to release the pain and hurt that came with our experiences and disconnect ourselves from a false image of trust. We need to change our understanding from what I call a human concept to a Divine concept. We need to step back into Divine Trust.

When we do that will we be able to rely on the Universe for guidance and unconditional support. We will be able to trust that prosperity and everything we need in order to receive it is already there for us.

༄༅

Meditation and Exercise:
Take a moment to check in with yourself. What do you believe about trust? Can you trust others? Can you trust yourself? Do you

trust in the guidance and unconditional love of the Universe? Write down any kind of negative associations you have with trust. Write down any phrases that you might have learned about trust (such as "I can trust no one").

Close your eyes and feel yourself surrounded by love and light. Ask to have any of those "old" ideas about trust to be released, and imagine them being transformed into unconditional love. Visualize any chords that are connecting you to people, places, and experiences associated with the "old" concept of trust being cut and transformed into unconditional love as well. Then visualize your understanding of trust shift from a human to a Divine concept. Feel that new energy of trust fill up every cell of your body.

Affirmation: "I now let go of any ideas about trust that no longer serve me and I move forward in the knowingness and concept of Divine Trust."

Day 29: Unlimited possibilities

In 1997 I did a twelve-week workshop based on the book The Artist's Way by Julia Cameron. On the first day of class our facilitator asked us, "What would you do if you had five million dollars in your bank account right now?" We all wrote down the most amazing things we wanted to do, since five million dollars seemed to give us unlimited possibilities. We shared it in class. We became excited. And then the question came up: but where do we get the five million dollars to live our dreams? Our teacher answered, "You can do anything you wrote down on that list without having five million dollars. Saying that you need the money first in order to follow your passions and manifest what you desire is an excuse for not starting at all. Just go out and do it. Opportunities will show up."

Very wise words! I still have my book from that class in 1997. And guess what? By 2003 I was doing pretty much all of the things from my list without having had the five million dollars first.

Our unconscious mind has an inborn security mechanism. We want guarantees to succeed before we start. We want to be financially secure before we move forward. We keep waiting for circumstances to be perfect before taking that next step; we hesitate taking that leap of faith, and we keep missing the unlimited possibilities that are waiting for us if we just had the courage to go for it.

The Universe is full of unlimited possibilities. All we need to do is connect to the energy of these unlimited possibilities. All we need to do is state what we want, believe that it is possible, and be open to receiving.

ஓஒ

Meditation and Exercise:
Take your notebook and answer the following questions: What would you do if you had all the money you needed? What would you start today if you had all the possibilities

you wanted? What would you do if you believed in unlimited prosperity? What would your life look like? What would you do if you knew you were unable to fail? Write down all the details. Do not limit yourself. Anything is possible, and you have the power to manifest it.

Close your eyes and center yourself in your heart chakra. Visualize a ball of light emanating from your heart and becoming bigger and bigger. It first encapsulates your physical body, then the room, the earth, and then the whole universe. Feel yourself connected to everything in existence. Feel yourself connected to all the possibilities you would like to have in your life, and feel yourself becoming one with them. Can you see now that everything you need is already there for you?

Affirmation: "I am now aware that I am a part of the unlimited possibilities of this Universe. I now know that everything I need is already there for me."

Day 30: Manifesting your future

Over the past thirty days you have explored and changed beliefs about prosperity from various perspectives. Have you felt a change in your life? Have you become aware of a new feeling of abundance? Do you now feel ready to accept the prosperity the Universe has in store for you?

Your future is happening right now. Whatever you are thinking and believing at this very moment is creating your future. Therefore, you have the power and the ability to create it the way you would like it to manifest.

Now that you have released old habits and beliefs about prosperity, the way is free to manifest what you desire.

It is very important that you keep up the good work you have been doing for the past thirty days and do not fall back into old patterns. Keep watching your thoughts. Be aware of your environment, the thoughts and beliefs of the people around you. Have discernment between their truth and your own truth.

Remember that everything you say, everything you think and any energy you send out creates your reality. Keep up the good thoughts. Keep blessing what you already have. And watch the miracles and the magic unfold in front of you!

༄༅

Meditation and Exercise:

Take a moment and think about where you would like to be a year from now. Write a mini bio. Write it in the now, as if you have already manifested everything. What would a perfect day in your life look like in a year from now? Where will you live? Who is going to be around you? How will you be spending your day? What are you doing in your life, now that prosperity has been allowed to manifest? Who are you, with this new sense of abundance? How will it feel to have all of this manifested in your life? Be as specific as you can, and don't limit yourself. Anything is possible in this abundant Universe.

Then close your eyes and visualize having everything manifested in your life. Become aware of the feelings associated with your manifestations.

Post your bio somewhere you can see it. Read it every morning before you start your day. The more you can get into a state of being the new you, of feeling what that life feels like, the faster it will manifest.

Be open to receiving. You deserve it!

Affirmation: "I am now open to receiving and living the prosperity of this Universe."

Continuing your journey

I invite you to continue this journey by signing a prosperity declaration. This declaration will help you to keep going into the direction that you started thirty days ago. It will remind you to keep positive thoughts and to be aware that you are connected to the prosperity available to you.

"I, _____, (write down your name) commit to continuing my journey to prosperity. Now that I am aware of the power of my thoughts, I will stay attentive and change any thought patterns that prevent my prosperity.

I now focus on thoughts that support good in my life, and on the blessings I receive. I will remember that I am a spark of Divine Source Energy, and that prosperity is always available for me. I choose prosperity in my life now."

Date it and sign it.

For another thirty days, focus on eliminating any other thoughts of lack that you become aware of. Whenever such a thought comes up, turn that thought immediately into a positive affirmation. If you keep doing this for thirty days, your life will take another quantum leap toward prosperity and the direction of your dreams.

Prologue

There is a Native American story in which a little boy asks his grandmother how long it will take for him to accomplish the task at hand. She says to him, "If you take your time, it will take a week. If you hurry up, it will take two weeks."

Take your path to prosperity one step, one thought, at a time. You don't have to push the river. Focus on being in the moment, instead of on how quickly you can reach your goals. Enjoy the journey. It is usually our joy and our love for the journey that will allow us to reach our goals—and often reach them faster than we could ever have imagined.

Much love and light to you!

Affirmations

Prosperity comes to me now with ease and grace.

Prosperity is my Divine birthright.

The prosperity in my life is an expression of my inner joy.

Prosperity is a gift to me from the Divine.

I am connected to the abundance of the Universe at all times.

I now accept abundance and prosperity in my life through means that bring me joy and emotional fulfillment, and that nurture my soul.

I give and receive with joy.

The Universe is the source of my Divine abundance.

I trust the Divine to provide for me at all times.

I deserve to live a life filled with joy, abundance, and prosperity.

I am connected to the unlimited possibilities of this Universe.

I now allow fun and play into every aspect of my life.

I am connected to a money concept that is based on love and joy.

Divine guidance leads me to prosperity and abundance. I am connected to and I trust that Divine guidance.

I am worthy and deserving of living a life filled with abundance.

Everything I need in order to create abundance and live my dreams is already available for me.

I am worthy and deserving of being abundant in every single aspect of my life.

My prosperity consciousness is unlimited.

I am grateful for the abundance in my life.

My inner guidance constantly leads me to new ways of abundance.

I know how to receive prosperity and abundance in the highest and best way for my highest and best good.

I now allow abundance, joy, and love to fill up every aspect of my life.

About the author

Kristie Reeves is an actress, producer and writer. Her mission is to create media that elevates the consciousness of the planet and sparks our divine truth.

Besides working in the entertainment industry, she has always had an interested in spiritual topics which led her to studying different healing modalities. She now includes that knowledge into the media she creates.

Kristie has been the producer and interviewer on "The Children of the Rainbow", a documentary series about empowering children and the gifts that new generation of children has for the world.

Kristie is also the host of Universal Broadcasting Network's radio show "Rebel Hearts w/ Kristie Reeves".

To find out more about Kristie's work please visit her website at
www.KristieReeves.com

This book is being published by Beurin Publishing, a subsidiary of Beurin Education and Beurin University. The mission of Beurin University is to educate and empower a new standard of heart-centered healer, uniting the wisdom and practices of ancient masters with our newest understandings of the body, mind and spirit.

Beurin Education and Beurin University is a non-profit, public benefit corporation for charitable purposes under section 501 (C) 3 IRS code, and the laws of the State of California.

To find out more about Beurin Education and Beurin University, visit our website at www.beurinuniversity.org

The author donates a portion of the profits of this book to charity.

www.ingramcontent.com/pod-product-compliance
Lightning Source LLC
Chambersburg PA
CBHW071722090426
42738CB00009B/1850